Dmitry Zenkin

The problem of inconsistency between law enforcement practice and labour law

AF294555

Dmitry Zenkin

The problem of inconsistency between law enforcement practice and labour law

ScienciaScripts

Imprint
Any brand names and product names mentioned in this book are subject to trademark, brand or patent protection and are trademarks or registered trademarks of their respective holders. The use of brand names, product names, common names, trade names, product descriptions etc. even without a particular marking in this work is in no way to be construed to mean that such names may be regarded as unrestricted in respect of trademark and brand protection legislation and could thus be used by anyone.

Cover image: www.ingimage.com

This book is a translation from the original published under ISBN 978-620-2-02375-7.

Publisher:
Sciencia Scripts
is a trademark of
Dodo Books Indian Ocean Ltd. and OmniScriptum S.R.L publishing group

120 High Road, East Finchley, London, N2 9ED, United Kingdom
Str. Armeneasca 28/1, office 1, Chisinau MD-2012, Republic of Moldova, Europe
Printed at: see last page
ISBN: 978-620-7-78442-4

Abstract: This article touches upon a very significant problem concerning conflicts and gaps in the current labour legislation. At present, reports in the mass media, statistical data of control and supervisory bodies on compliance with labour legislation and other normative legal acts containing norms of labour law in our country still indicate very unfavourable trends in the field of observance of labour rights of citizens of the Russian Federation.

Keywords: Collisions, gaps, labour legislation, labour code, labour relations.

Introduction

The relevance of this topic is due to the fact that in modern economic conditions there is a lot of talk about negative phenomena in Russian labour law. Their presence is obvious. They include a certain blurring of the subject matter of the branch, attempts to justify the "absorption" of labour law by civil law, attributing only to administrative law the relations of public service, the decline in the role of trade unions and individualisation of labour relations, the quantitative growth of "atypical", not fitting into the classical scheme of labour relations and increasing "flexibility" of employment. These new and rather unfavourable trends for labour law also need theoretical analysis, primarily through the provisions of the general part of labour law. Simply ignoring these problems or mechanically denying them can only negativise the situation.

In market conditions, contracts in labour law become one of the most important problems of the science of labour law. It is no longer possible to study it only from the traditional positions of the labour contract. Consequently, new, general theoretical approaches are needed, taking into account modern achievements of the theory of contracts.

The science and practice of labour law has accumulated sufficient material to define a contract and its types. A contract in labour law is an agreement of two or more subjects aimed at establishing, changing or terminating relations that constitute the subject matter of labour law. In this sense, a contract will be a regional, territorial, sectoral, as well as all other agreements that formalise the modification of a labour legal relationship, for example, in connection with a change in the technical or social organisation of labour (on transfers, on the establishment of part-time working hours). Consequently, contracts in labour law are numerous bilateral and trilateral social and labour transactions. A contract in labour law takes place where and when the expression of the will of legally equal subjects of labour law recognised by the state in a particular situation is aimed at establishing, changing or reducing social and labour relations.
- of labour relations.

Labour law distinguishes between individual and collective agreements and a whole system of agreements, for example, mediating the results of social and labour relations in the sphere of wage labour.

The relevance of the study of the theory of contracts in labour law cannot but affect its system. The development of such theory and generalisation of the practice of social partnership will allow, for example, to solve the issue of the place of collective bargaining and agreements in the general and special parts of modern Russian labour law. Moreover, since the types of contracts in labour law are not exhausted by the content of the Labour Code of the Russian Federation in the General Part of Labour Law, there is already a sufficient number of norms that can be combined into the institute of labour transactions. This institute may include norms on the concept of contracts, their legally significant form, types, conditions of validity, etc. And in many respects it is up to the representatives of the science of labour law and the legislator to formalize them in the form of a separate chapter (or chapters) of the Labour Code of the Russian Federation.

The object of research of this topic is the relations arising in the sphere of social and labour legal relations, labour legal relations.

The subject of the study is the rules of law governing these relations.

The purpose of this paper is the legal analysis of the institute of labour contract, consideration of theoretical and practical problems arising in labour legal relations related to the current legislation.

In order to achieve the above objective, the following tasks are proposed:

- to disclose the legal aspects of concluding a contract;

- Analyse the grounds for changing the employment contract and the problems of law enforcement practice in the field of labour law relations

- Identify patterns and shortcomings in the conclusion and termination of the labour contract, determine the guarantees of legal protection.

The methodological basis of the study of this topic includes: the method of legal analysis, comparative - legal method, systemic - functional.

Theoretical basis of the study are scientific works: Alexandrov N.G., Alekseev S.S., Bondarenko E.N., Lebedev V.M., Sinitsin A.N..

Currently, the system of labour law in Russia is most fully reflected in the Labour Code of the Russian Federation. Therefore, the study of the labour law system is primarily related to the study of the structure and content of this codified legislative act. Along with the system of labour law and the system of labour legislation, there is also the system of the science of labour law - a set of theoretical views, judgments and conclusions concerning the problems of legal regulation of social relations in the sphere of application and organization of labour.

Chapter 1 The employment contract as a central institution of labour law

Concept and characteristics of labour law

All employees in the Russian Federation exercise their rights by voluntarily concluding an employment contract. At the same time, an employment contract is also a legal fact of exercising other rights and obligations of employees to work in good faith in their chosen field of activity. An employment contract can be distinguished in three aspects 1) as an agreement to work as an employee; 2) as a legal fact, which is the basis for the emergence and form of existence of a labour legal relationship in time and serves as a prerequisite for the emergence and existence of other legal relationships closely related to labour relations; 3) as an institute of labour law, i.e. a system of legal norms on hiring (conclusion of an employment contract), transfer to another job and dismissal.

According to Article 56 of the Labour Code of the Russian Federation, an employment contract is an agreement between an employee and an employer, under which the employee undertakes to perform work in a certain specialty, qualification or position subject to internal labour regulations, and the employer undertakes to pay the employee on a specified date and in full wages and to ensure working conditions stipulated by the labour legislation, collective agreement and agreement of the parties.

This definition shows the characteristic features of an employment contract, which allow to distinguish it from related civil law contracts (contract for work, assignment, commission, publishing contract, etc.), the content of which is also labour activity. Under civil law contracts, the employee's obligation is related to the performance of specific individual work. A labour contract provides for the employee's subordination to internal labour regulations. At the conclusion of civil law contracts the process is not regulated, the performer distributes the time of work at his discretion, and the relationship of the parties arises only in relation to the result of labour. Therefore, not every labour agreement is

with a labour contract.

For example, under a contract of hire, the contractor on behalf of the customer undertakes to carry out certain work at his own risk using his own or the customer's materials within a specified period of time, and the customer accepts and pays for the work. Most often this work is of a one-off nature and can take place anywhere and at any time, not necessarily at the customer's location and during working hours. The contractor is not bound by the mode, schedule or measure of labour. All these matters are at his discretion.

Closely related to the contract of employment is the labour agreement, under which the company undertakes to pay the employee wages at predetermined wage rates, salaries, for a certain amount of products produced or a certain amount of working time.

An employment contract is an ordinary fixed-term employment contract and may be concluded in the usual form, i.e. by submitting an application to the employer for employment for a certain period of time or for the performance of a certain work or by drawing up a fixed-term employment contract.

The subject of an employment contract is the personal performance of a labour function in the general labour process of a given production team, i.e. daily labour activity, manifestation of physical and mental energy of an employee in a particular specialty, qualification, position in the general labour process of a given labour team. Consequently, the subject of the labour contract is the very live labour of the employee in the general process of production as a manifestation in time of his general and special working capacity. The subject of related civil contracts is the embodied end result of labour (invention, painting, etc.), and labour in them is only a way of fulfilling the undertaken obligations. Subordination of the employee in the process of performing the labour function to the rules of internal labour regulations with the performance of the established measure of labour. For violation of this obligation, he may bear disciplinary responsibility, which is not the case in civil law contracts.

The obligation of an enterprise, institution or organisation to organise the work of an employee, to create normal working conditions for him, to provide him daily with conditional work, to protect his health and life in the process of work, to reward him systematically for actual work according to predetermined norms.

In the science of labour law the labour contract is considered as a form of implementation of the right to work, the basis for the emergence and implementation of labour legal relations, a legal institute that combines the norms on the emergence, change and termination of labour rights and obligations [8, p.111].

The most important feature of the institute of the labour contract, which permeates both the norms of the law on recruitment and the norms on transfers and dismissal, is the freedom of the labour contract, reflecting the principle of freedom of labour in society, enshrined in Article 37 of the Constitution of the Russian Federation. Freedom of labour contract means that citizens: a) freely, at their will, choose the place and kind of labour activity, work; b) freely, voluntarily decide the issue of work, conclude a labour contract and can terminate it at any time in the manner prescribed by law; c) have, as a rule, stable labour contracts. The labour contract reflects the contractual principle of employment as an employee.

In legal science, the labour contract is considered, first of all, as an abstract category. This approach is quite legitimate and understandable from a normativist position. However, the labour contract cannot be considered as a certain "monolith", i.e. as a single whole concept that is not subject to differentiation. In the interests of theory, and even more so in the interests of practice, it is advisable to distinguish between the hypostases of the labour contract, not to combine them together without taking into account the purpose to which it is directed, and, consequently, to distinguish in such cases its specific functions. In other words, it is always fruitful to concretise the labour contract as an abstraction, taking into account its objectives and functions ensuring their achievement.

Like any legal relationship, an employment contract has content, generated by the mutual reciprocal agreement of its parties. The content of any contract is understood as its terms and conditions. They determine the rights and obligations of the parties. The content of a labour contract is a set of its terms and conditions. These terms of the contract determine the rights and obligations of the parties. Meanwhile, it is necessary to distinguish between the content of the labour contract, which means all its terms and conditions, and the content of the labour legal relationship, i.e. the rights and obligations of its subjects. Determined by the employment contract and labour legislation. Each party to an employment contract has its own subjective rights and obligations spelled out in the contract and established by labour legislation. Depending on the established procedure, there may be differences between the two conditions of the contract: a direct, established by the agreement of the parties at the conclusion of the labour contract   ;

b derivative, established by the parties' agreement at the conclusion of the labour contract   ;   b derivative, established by the parties' agreement at the conclusion of the labour contract.

These conditions are defined by the legislation (labour protection, disciplinary and material liability, etc., which may be changed by agreement of the parties (unless otherwise provided by law). Therefore, the parties do not agree on derivative conditions, knowing that with the conclusion of the contract, these conditions are already binding by virtue of the law and the contract (under which the parties have undertaken to obey the internal labour regulations of production). Formulation of a certain type of conditions in the employment contract, establishment of legal guarantees of their performance has a positive impact on the implementation of the educational role of the employment contract.

Thus, information conditions allow the employer to get acquainted in advance with the conditions of labour, its payment and protection, guarantees of their observance, established in the law, collective agreement, agreements, local normative legal acts. This block of conditions is directly related to the labour discipline of the hirer, his conscientious attitude to the performance of his labour function. In this case, there is a well-founded regularity: the wider the range of information conditions, the more information about his future work the hirer receives, the less he will allow violations of the rules of labour behaviour, the less he will learn the prohibitions and permissions in the process of production of methods of "trial and error", which is usually associated with violation of the requirements of internal regulations. The block of analysed conditions also includes such conditions that are not directly related to the labour process. For example, the condition of compulsory social insurance may be stated not only in the form of a reference to the Labour Code of the Russian Federation and other federal laws, but also by including in the employment contract an extract from the legislation relevant to the performance of the employee's labour function. The educational function of information conditions is ensured by the norm stipulated in Part H of Article 68 of the Labour Code of the Russian Federation. The legislator obliges the employer at the time of hiring (before signing the employment contract) to familiarise the hirer against signature with the internal labour regulations, other local normative legal acts directly related to the employee's work activity, the collective agreement of the organisation.

The immediate conditions determined by the agreement of the parties, establish a greater and or lesser scope of rights and obligations of the parties. For example, by agreement of the parties, the work may be defined as part-time or home-based, or be temporary, etc. Necessary conditions of the contract determine the emergence of labour legal relations, reflecting all conditions of labour established by law and agreement of the parties. Обязательными и существенными условиями договора определяются конкретное место работы (с указанием соответствующего структурного подразделения организации), дата начала работы, наименование специальности, профессии, должности, которую будет занимать работник, права и обязанности работника и работодателя, условия о характере трудовой функции (т.е. на какой должности и какую конкретную работу гражданин будет выполнять, специфика трудовой деятельности и др.), условия о времени действия трудового договора (т.е. заключен ли договор на какой-то определен

When we speak of the duties, for example, of an official, we mean the degree of responsibility imposed on him. However, the position also defines the employee's powers, which he or she is entitled to use. An unambiguous definition of duties and powers in the employment contract allows the employer to organise work efficiently, provides the employee with certainty about his/her functions, and gives the two parties the opportunity to resolve disputes without conflict. In practice, it happens that in order to simplify the form (text) of the employment contract, the employer seeks to set out the maximum duties and powers of the employee (labour function) in job descriptions.

This fact is currently taking place. A rather saturated unemployed labour market creates certain tension in negotiations and the procedure of concluding an employment contract. On the one hand, the labour contract allows the employer to make a qualitative selection of the labour force, but on the other hand, it creates certain conditions for the employer's arbitrariness. As practice shows, the employer usually dictates to the hirer its own terms of employment, which it formulates in advance in a standard draft labour contract already prepared without the hirer's participation, inviting the latter to sign it or terminate further negotiations. The current labour legislation contains the necessary legal guarantees, according to which it would be possible for an employee to challenge the content of the employment contract without the risk of losing his job or "spoiling" his relationship with the employer. The way out of the seemingly deadlocked situation should be sought not only in improving labour legislation, as it is always powerless if the addressee, who is the target of the legal norm, will try to resolve their conflicts with the employer "one on one".

The professional association of workers, including at the level of the organisation, needs to be restructured accordingly. Its goal should not be the collection of trade union dues and maintenance of a superior bureaucratic apparatus, but the defence of the interests and rights of a member of the trade union society. Not every single employee should have a conflict with the employer, but the head of the trade union, starting from its primary level, is obliged to keep a finger on the pulse of labour relations between the employee and the employer and its representatives without the employee's participation, on his own initiative. If the need arises, it is also necessary to appeal to the Labour Commission, the court, seeking to eliminate violations of labour rights, interests of both individual employees and a certain collective. Therefore, an employee should make sure that these instructions are properly executed and, if necessary, their legal force cannot be questioned Labour attitude, choice of labour behaviour, i.e. the attitude of a hired employee to his work, production team, organisation in market conditions of economic management cannot be assessed unambiguously. The point is that any labour contract is a means of socialisation of an individual, whose interests and talents can also manifest themselves in the activities of the labour collective, its bodies, i.e. in the sphere of protection of the interests of employees, in the management of the enterprise.

Socialisation of the employee is an important factor in its formation. It can be noted from the following that the main purpose of the labour contract is to give effect to the norm of objective law.

Its main function is to perform the role of a labour transaction, a legal fact to which the legislator binds the emergence of labour rights and obligations, i.e. a labour legal relationship. The auxiliary purpose of the employment contract and, accordingly, its function is to perform the role of a document, the function of fulfilling mutual rights and obligations.

1.1   Legal aspects of concluding and amending an employment contract

Current labour legislation establishes a certain procedure for hiring, concluding an employment contract, and documenting them.

In today's environment, employers have different approaches to the issue of formalising employment, sometimes going to one extreme or another. In one case, employment is not formalised in any way, forgetting that actual admission to work entails the same consequences as documented employment. In the other case, various certificates, questionnaires, characteristics, recommendations are required from the job seeker. Of course, in each specific case, the employer has the right to establish a list of documents to be submitted at the time of hiring in its own interests.

The constitutional provision that labour is free, everyone has the right to freely dispose of his or her abilities to work, to choose an occupation and profession, and to have equal opportunities when concluding a contract is the basic principle of legal regulation of labour relations. This principle is manifested in various articles of the Labour Code, most notably in article 64, which is devoted to guarantees in concluding a labour contract. This article prohibits unjustified refusal to conclude a labour contract. Thus, any refusal to conclude an employment contract is considered a refusal if it is not based on an assessment of the business qualities of the person applying for the job.

Business qualities mean the ability of a natural person to perform a certain labour function taking into account his/her professional qualifications (e.g. a certain profession, special qualifications), personal qualities of an employee (e.g. health condition, a certain level of education, work experience in a given speciality in a given industry). In addition, along with standard or typical professional qualification requirements, the employer has the right to impose additional requirements necessary for the performance of labour functions (e.g. proficiency in one or more foreign languages, computer skills).

Article 64 of the Labour Code states that refusal to conclude a labour contract may be appealed in court. Such an appeal is allowed in case of refusal to conclude an employment contract on the grounds listed in Article 64 of the Labour Code (which prohibits refusal to conclude an employment contract for women on grounds related to pregnancy or the presence of children, and for employees invited in writing to work as a transfer from another employer - within one month from the date of dismissal from the previous place of work), and on other grounds related to the assessment of the employee's business qualities. The court, having established only the fact of refusal to conclude an employment contract on the grounds stipulated in Article 64 of the Labour Code, decides to conclude an employment contract with the employee. If the court finds that the refusal to hire an employee on the grounds of the employee's lack of business qualities is justified, the employee's claim to conclude a labour contract with him or her cannot be satisfied.

Resolution of the Plenum of the Supreme Court of the Russian Federation of 17 March 2004 No. 2 drew the attention of the courts to the fact that the employer's refusal to conclude an employment contract with a person who has a job, on the grounds of his lack of registration at the place of residence, stay or location is not legal. Such refusal violates the right of citizens to freedom of movement, choice of place of stay and residence guaranteed by the Constitution of the Russian Federation (part 1 of article 27), the Law of the Russian Federation of 25 June 1993 No. 5242-1 "On the right of citizens of the Russian Federation to freedom of movement, choice of place of stay and residence within the Russian Federation", and also contradicts part 2 of article 64 of the Labour Code, which prohibits restricting rights or establishing any advantages when concluding an employment contract on the above grounds.

Thus, the numerous announcements by employers in Moscow and the Moscow region that persons with registration in Moscow and the Moscow region are required to work discriminate against the rights of job seekers and may be the subject of proceedings by the labour inspectorate and the prosecutor's office, since article 136 of the Criminal Code provides for liability (up to and including imprisonment) for violation of the equality of rights of citizens, including on the basis of place of residence. Article 145 of the Criminal Code also provides for liability for unjustified refusal to hire or unjustified dismissal of a pregnant woman or a woman with children under the age of 3. In view of the foregoing, the courts, when considering cases involving the challenge of a refusal to hire and having established that a citizen's rights have been violated, must inform the relevant procurator of that fact by issuing a private ruling and point out to the employer the inadmissibility of violating citizens' rights.

When considering cases of refusal to conclude a labour contract, the courts must take into account the employer's explanations that he has given to the employee in writing. At the request of a person who is refused to conclude a labour contract, the employer is obliged to provide the reason for the refusal in writing; this provision is an innovation in the Labour Code.

Labour legislation contains a list of grounds when a refusal to accept a job is considered unreasonable. However, this list is not exhaustive, and practice supplements it. Unjustified refusal to hire a worker can be appealed directly in court.

In judicial practice abroad, special attention is paid to discrimination in hiring, discussing the problem of reliability or, business qualities of an employee in the workplace, as well as the criteria for its assessment. Direct, deliberate, secret or non-obvious, indirect discrimination is widespread in the hiring process in the Russian Federation as well. The current legislation (article 37 of the Constitution of the Russian Federation, articles 2, 3, 64, 261 of the Labour Code of the Russian Federation) does not provide a mechanism for identifying and proving discrimination in hiring and protecting the labour rights and interests of job applicants violated in such cases. Nor does paragraph 1O of Resolution No. 63 of the Plenum of the Supreme Court of the Russian Federation "On introducing amendments and additions to Resolution No. 2 of the Plenum of the Supreme Court of the Russian Federation of 17 March 2004 "On the application by the courts of the Russian Federation of the Labour Code of the Russian Federation" fill these gaps.

The Supreme Court clarifies that when considering labour disputes relating to refusal of employment, it must be borne in mind that labour is free and everyone has the right to freely dispose of his or her abilities to work, to choose an occupation and profession, and to have equal opportunities in concluding an employment contract without any discrimination, i.e. any direct or indirect restriction of rights or the establishment of direct or indirect advantages in concluding an employment contract on the basis of sex, race, colour, nationality, race, skin colour or nationality. [25, c.97].

Meanwhile, in cases of this category, in order to optimally reconcile the interests of the employer and the person wishing to conclude a labour contract, and taking into account the fact that. Based on the content of Art. 8, Part 1 of Art. 34, Part 1 and 2 of Art. 35 of the Constitution of the Russian Federation and Paragraph 5 of Part 1 of Art. 1 and 2 of Article 35 of the Constitution of the Russian Federation and paragraph 5 of Part 1 of Article 22 of the Labour Code of the Russian Federation, for the purposes of effective economic activity and rational management of property, the employer independently, under its own responsibility, makes the necessary personnel decisions (recruitment, placement and dismissal of personnel) and the conclusion of an employment contract with a particular job-seeker is the right and not the obligation of the employer, as well as the fact that the Code does not contain norms obliging the employer to fill vacant positions or jobs immediately as they arise, it is necessary to check whether the employer has the right to fill vacant positions or jobs as soon as they arise.

The employer must check whether the person in question has been offered a vacancy (e.g. a vacancy notice has been submitted to the employment service, placed in a newspaper, advertised on the radio, announced during speeches to graduates, posted on a notice board), whether negotiations for employment have been conducted with the person in question and on what grounds he or she has been refused a labour contract.

The above explanation of the Supreme Court already contains a contradiction. If it is the employer's right and not the employer's obligation to conclude a labour contract, then any reasoning that an employer cannot refuse to hire an employee at any stage of concluding a labour contract if there is strong evidence of refusal due to circumstances of a discriminatory nature or unrelated to the employee's business qualities is meaningless.

The employer, in cases falling under discrimination and in cases based on a non-business evaluation of the quality of the applicant, may announce at any stage of the conclusion of the labour contract that he/she is terminating negotiations with the applicant, considering it more appropriate to leave the place of work vacant for an indefinite period of time and referring to Article 35 of the Constitution of the Russian Federation and Article 22.1 of the Labour Code of the Russian Federation.

If there is a vacancy, to provide work, to take care of reducing unemployment is still not a right, but a civil obligation of the employer. In market conditions of economic management this provision should be enshrined not only in the moral law, but also in the legal law as the most important mission of the employer in the Russian civil society.

Labour legislation establishes health protection guarantees for women and adolescents at the time of employment, taking into account the physiological peculiarities of the adolescent body, which require special protection against certain occupational hazards not yet known to the person in question at the time of employment.

The labour contract should be in written form, drawn up in two copies (if the law or other normative legal act   that the labour contract is concluded in does not provide for the drawing up of more copies). It should be borne in mind that the labour contract is in writing and is drawn up in two copies (unless the law or other normative legal act provides for the drawing up of labour contracts in more copies), each of which is signed by the parties. One copy of the labour contract is given to the employee. The employee's receipt of a copy of the labour contract must be confirmed by the employee's signature on the copy of the labour contract kept by the employer.

We cannot ignore another problem related to the conclusion of the contract. An elementary analysis of Article 57 of the Labour Code of the Russian Federation allows us to question whether it contains only rights or a number of conditions mediating the obligations of the parties, developed by them jointly. In other words, the labour contract also contains joint conditions binding on both parties. In such cases, each of the parties has the right to demand the fulfilment of such a condition by the other party (to stipulate in the contract the date of commencement of work, working hours and rest periods, etc.).

The procedure of employment should be distinguished from the conclusion of a labour contract. Employment is formalised by an order of the company's administration, which is announced to the employee against signature.

In practice, there is a widespread opinion that the order not only formalises a specific labour legal relationship, but also gives rise to it. In fact, the order on employment is issued after the worker expresses his/her desire to work at a given enterprise under the proposed conditions, and therefore is not a law-forming fact, but only accompanies the conclusion of the contract. A citizen may start work on the basis of a verbal order from the administration. Moreover, the actual admission to work is considered to be the conclusion of a labour contract regardless of whether the employment was duly formalised (but provided that the work was performed on the instructions or with the knowledge of the official with the right to hire). At the same time, the order is the main document determining the legal status of a citizen in the structure of the labour collective, the legal basis (along with other conditions) for making wage settlements and other legally significant actions.

Thus, by concluding a contract, a person who wants to get a job agrees to join a production team that already has its own traditions and rules of labour behaviour. In other words, he or she as a person consciously goes to limit his or her ambitions, trying to self-realise in the conditions offered to him or her by the employer. Psychologically, it is a rather complex and contradictory process of coordination, subordination of interests, their realisation or, on the contrary, their sacrifice, when, for the sake of material well-being, the hired person, figuratively speaking, suppresses, or maybe loses his talent, his abilities, refusing to realise them, to develop them in time, because the work he performs takes away his time and strength. Such "losers" are very common in reality. Successes and failures of an employee in similar cases are explained first of all by peculiarities of personality psychology (character, temperament, abilities, etc.). Nowadays it is more and more often possible to meet a teacher who trades in the market, an engineer who provides one-time services in the household, an agronomist engaged in housekeeping, etc.

A sufficiently saturated unemployed labour market creates certain tension in negotiations and the procedure of concluding an employment contract. On the one hand, the labour contract allows the employer to make a qualitative selection of labour force, but on the other hand it creates certain conditions for the employer's arbitrariness.

Analysis of the basis for amending an employment contract

An employment contract is usually a motivated volitional act of the subject(s) of labour law. " The will and its motives constitute the inner side of a legal transaction". The analysis of labour contracts makes it possible to state that the legislator does not treat the motive indifferently. In a number of cases, it is the specific motive that determines the direction and content of this act of the subject of labour law. Thus, in accordance with Article 73 of the Labour Code of the Russian Federation, the employer unilaterally changes the essential working conditions in connection with organisational or technological changes, offering the employee to accept or dismiss them. In such a case, the specific motivation determines the focus and content of the labour contract-transfer of the employee. Such an approach to the analysis of the labour contract allows us to identify the internal (subjective) side of the labour contract legally significant motives and will of its parties. [25 c.125]

In the science of the labour contract, the content of the labour contract is usually understood as its terms and conditions: direct, which are established by the agreement of the parties at its conclusion. And derivative ones established in the current legislation on labour. Thus, to the content of the labour contract N.G. Aleksandrov did not include the rights and obligations of the parties. Moreover, he pointed out that the labour contract serves as a basis for the emergence of a labour legal relationship.

A.D. Zaikin, quoting Article 15 of the Labour Code of the RF, made two conclusions from its analysis: 1) a labour contract is an agreement of the parties aimed at establishing a labour legal relationship between them. In this case, the employment contract performs the role of a legal fact - a labour transaction (actions of the parties); 2) the employment contract defines the main duties of its parties, i.e. it performs the function of a labour legal relationship, since each legal duty of one party corresponds to the corresponding power of the other party. Such conclusions are incorrect, because a labour contract cannot simultaneously perform two different functions in one and the same, i.e. in a specific mechanism of legal regulation of certain labour relations - a legal fact and a legal relationship [26, p.54].

When analysing the content of an employment contract, it is quite reasonable to stress that it is necessary to distinguish between the content of an employment contract and the content of an employment legal relationship. If the former can be understood as

all conditions, the second is the rights and obligations of its subjects. Another statement on the content of a labour contract is also possible: "The content of a labour contract is the mutual obligations of the parties". The rights and obligations of the employee and the employer are included in the content of the labour contract.

The science of Russian labour law has a long tradition of mixing contract and obligation. Back in 1938, A.N. Finogenov argued that a labour contract "fixes and specifies mutual obligations and rights of an employee with the administration of an enterprise (institution, farm).

Subsequently, the science of labour law has repeatedly pointed out the possibility of contractual changes in working conditions. However, the relevant agreement between the employer and the employee was not regarded as independent, i.e. along with the employment contract. As a rule, it was about changing the labour function within the limits of the concluded employment contract. In other words, if the parties mutually agreed to change the content of the employment function, such a transaction was not recognised as independent and was considered to have been made within the framework of the previous employment contract.

It is quite obvious that in the science of labour law the cult of a single, all-powerful employment contract that lasts for the entire period of employment of an employee in a particular organisation until its official termination and only on the grounds provided for in the current labour legislation is firmly entrenched. Such a labour contract as an abstraction is in clear contradiction with practice. This can be illustrated by one of the numerous examples [27 p. 32].

Thus, Lebedev concluded a labour contract with LLC MC REGION, under which he was hired as a fitter in shop No. 1 of the joint-stock company. Two years later, after graduating from the Polytechnic University, Lebedev was transferred to shop No. 2 as a foreman. The transfer was formalised by the order of the director of LLC MC "REGION", with which Lebedev was familiarised, agreed with its content, about which he made the following entry: "I am familiarised with the order. I agree with the transfer. Lebedev." The following year Lebedev, also with his consent, was transferred as deputy director to a branch of LLC Management Company REGION, located in another city. However, he was unable to perform his new job function properly and was warned of his dismissal for incompatibility with his position. Lebedev did not dispute the grounds for his dismissal, as he was convinced that he did not have sufficient knowledge of economics and marketing to fulfil the duties of deputy director of the branch. Considering himself to be an excellent engineer, he demanded to be reinstated as a foreman of workshop No. 2 of LLC MC REGION. Since all engineering positions in the joint-stock company refused to be filled, the director of the joint-stock company offered Lebedev, until a vacancy for an engineering position appeared, to transfer to the job specified in his labour contract - as a fitter of shop No. 1 of LLC MC REGION. Lebedev refused such a transfer and was dismissed for incompatibility with his position.

If in the above example we proceed from the well-known provision that only a labour contract is the basis for the emergence and existence of a specific labour legal relationship in time, then the proposal of the director of the limited liability company MC REGION to Lebedev can be considered to a certain extent justified, although its absurdity from a practical point of view is quite obvious. When transferring to another job Lebedev with the joint-stock company arose a new labour legal relationship, the rights and obligations of the parties to which did not even remotely resemble the content of the former. The legal fact for its emergence was the transfer agreement. Only the parties to the previous labour legal relationship remained in the case of transfers. In this connection, it would be appropriate to note that the subject of the primary labour legal relationship - fitter Lebedev - differed in its legally significant characteristics from Lebedev - shop manager or deputy director of the branch of LLC MC REGION. An employee in a labour legal relationship is not only a natural person exercising his/her labour legal personality, but also a performer possessing the relevant, necessary for the performance of a specific labour function.

When N.G. Aleksandrov defined the labour contract as the basis for the emergence of a "concrete ..... labour legal relationship" and its existence in time, he meant not an abstraction, but a concrete labour legal relationship with a completely defined range of powers and duties of the parties. At present, this position is often ignored by researchers of this problem. Such a position of the science of labour law to some extent would be justified, but only in the context of the theory of a single and indivisible labour legal relationship. A completely justified rejection of it requires a revision of the grounds for the emergence of labour legal relations, including in their number and other agreements of the employer and the employee, for example, the agreement on transfers. Transfer is an agreement between the employer and the employee, which not only modifies (clarifies, changes) the existing labour legal relationship by the time of reaching an agreement on transfer, but may also be the basis for the emergence of a new one, if it is a question of changing a critical mass of necessary conditions of the existing employment contract. And this cannot be disregarded. As it was shown in the case of Lebedev, the position of the modern science of labour law in this part does not agree with practice. The specific legal relationship that has arisen again after Lebedev's next transfer to another job is indeed a continuing one. But the basis of its existence in time will not be Lebedev's agreement with LLC MC "REGION" on the work of a fitter, but their next transfer agreement. Consequently, it is incorrect to reduce the grounds for the emergence, change and termination of a labour legal relationship and other closely related relations to only one labour transaction - a labour agreement.

contract. Its role can be performed by other labour transactions. [4, c.237-238.]

At present, as already noted, the theory of transactions is studied by the science of civil law. In the Russian legal science this position was established in the Soviet period. In the theory of Russian law before 1917. The qualification of actions as legal facts included their two types: transactions and offences. "Under the name of a legal transaction, - wrote G.F. Shershevich (no longer as a civilist, as a theorist), - is understood such a legal consequence, connected by law with this fact".

The preservation of the institute of transactions in civil law allowed civilists to systematically fix all types of contracts, conditions and forms of their performance, consequences of violation of the form and, most importantly, to regulate the invalidity of contracts (voidable and voidable transactions, consequences of invalidity of the transaction, etc.). These are the problems that are directly related to labour transactions, but which have not been properly regulated in labour law and have not yet been sufficiently investigated by the science of labour law.

In connection with the above, I would like to make a few general theoretical remarks. Mention of the common roots of labour and civil law should not be associated with attempts to absorb labour law into civil law, with its "dissolution" in civil law. The period of historical assessment of the mentioned unity should already be replaced by a reasonable study of possible cross-fertilisation of these branches of law, their subsidiary interdependence. Thus. It makes no sense for civil law to develop its own, for example, such concepts used in the Civil Code of the Russian Federation as "employer", "employee", "minimum wage", "salary", etc. At the same time, it is difficult to speak, for example, about the details of a power of attorney to receive wages, about the employer as a legal entity, about a bonded or sham labour contract and other invalid transactions, without currently referring to the relevant norms of civil law. Solving the problems of subsidiary application of civil law norms in labour law should lead not to the unification of these branches, but, on the contrary, to a more detailed development of individual institutes of labour law.

In the literature on labour law there are both supporters and opponents of labour transactions. M.V. Lushnikova, A.M. Lushnikov spoke out against the use of the term "labour transaction" as a generic concept: " We propose to single out labour contracts as a generic concept". We could agree with this proposal if we study only the labour contract. It is hardly possible to refer a collective agreement and all types of agreements (Article 45 of the Labour Code of the RF) to labour contracts without significant reservations. The fact is that these labour transactions contain a number of provisions that are really made by subjects of labour law, but, as already noted, have a very indirect relation to labour (observance of the interests of employees in the privatisation of the organisation, departmental housing; ensuring environmental safety; health improvement and recreation of employees and members of their families, especially children, etc.). [23, c.62-63].

Moreover, labour contracts are specific not only to labour law but also to civil law.

It is impossible not to agree with the conclusion of M. V. Lushnikova and A. M. Lushnikov that "the most relevant is the development of a branch doctrine of contracts". But at the same time, the refusal to develop a branch generic concept that unites all types of contracts and agreements in labour law is obviously a stumbling block to achieve this goal. [23 c.32].

In conclusion, it should be noted once again that, proposing to use the term "labour transaction" as a generic concept does not identify its civil law concept of a transaction. Thus, the coincidence in form of differentiation of labour transactions into unilateral, multilateral and bilateral does not mean that in labour law one should not look for their inherent features. In particular, labour law cannot define transactions exclusively as lawful actions of subjects of labour law.

Not only before the conclusion of a labour contract, but also in the course of labour activity, it is wrong to deny subjects of labour law, as they say, from the outset in the autonomy of will and equality of rights. It is time to reconsider the view of the employee as a powerless, weak-willed subject, crushed by the arbitrariness of the employer. This is not always and everywhere true. A number of examples can be cited in support of the above. Thus, both the employee and the employer may refuse to transfer to another job, and this does not mean that such actions will definitely lead to disciplinary liability or dismissal. An employee may refuse to receive a one-off incentive. He, as a party to such a transaction, has no corresponding obligation. Why can't the actions of an employer providing an employee with a measure of material or moral encouragement be called a unilateral labour transaction? Why should the refusal to participate in a strike be considered a bilateral or multilateral labour contract, and not a unilateral or multilateral labour contract, and not a unilateral labour-law transaction? We will never develop our theory of transactions if we constantly try on the caftan of civil law theory. The proposal to use "labour contracts" as a generic concept today no longer reflects labour-law realities. It cannot be used productively in the study of, for example, labour law agreements, collective bargaining agreements, i.e. it leaves out of the research field a significant part of labour transactions in market conditions of economic management.

It will be appropriate to repeat once again: if one does not like the term "labour transaction" or if one cannot fulfil the role of a generic concept in the science of labour law "labour contracts", one should look for other options. Only a simple denial of already published developments on this subject is not the best way to develop the foundations of contractual labour law in Russia, in other words,
theories of labour transactions.

1.2 Problem of law enforcement practice in the field of labour law
legal relations regulating the labour contract

The content of an employment contract is characterised by the fact that each employee, in accordance with the employment contract, is obliged to ensure the performance of work in a certain speciality (position) and to bear personal responsibility for it.

However, due to objective and subjective factors (reconstruction of the organisation, changes in production, improvement of the employee's qualifications, supply disruptions, etc.), sometimes it becomes impossible or unnecessary for the employee to perform the work function specified at the time of employment. In such cases, the legislation allows for the transfer of employees to another job.

Since the agreement on the work function is one of the most important conditions of the labour contract, transfer to another job may be associated with a change in a set of labour rights and obligations relating to the procedure of remuneration, the right to leave, the calculation of length of service, the condition of pension provision, etc. In other words, transfer to another job affects the essential rights and interests of workers. Thus, other work not stipulated in the agreement, not corresponding to the speciality, qualification or position stipulated in the agreement. Assignment to a worker of work that does not correspond to his qualifications established at the time of employment, even if within the boundaries of the specified type of activity, should also be considered a transfer to another job, requiring the consent of the employee [28, p.84].

Other work, i.e. work not stipulated in the agreement, is any work that does not correspond to the speciality, qualification or position stipulated in the agreement. Assignment of a worker to work that does not correspond to his/her qualifications established at the time of employment, even if within the scope of the specified type of activity, should also be considered a transfer to another job, requiring a change in the employment contract.

The employer may not require the employee to perform work outside the subdivision and workplace, if they are not stipulated in the contract, as well as outside the location of the enterprise, except in cases of business trips to perform certain tasks outside the place of permanent work. Assignment of work in another locality, as well as transfer of an employee to another locality, at least together with the enterprise (institution, organisation), is a transfer to another job, if work in another locality was not conditioned in the employment contract or does not arise from the content of the employee's work function.

The departmental subordination of the enterprise is irrelevant when characterising the place of work, because its transfer from the subordination of one body to another does not terminate the employment contract. However, in the event of a change of ownership, merger, division or consolidation of enterprises, the subject of the contract, the condition of the place of work is changed and therefore labour relations continue only with the consent of the employee; termination of the employment contract on the initiative of the employer in these cases is possible only in the case of a reduction in the number or staff of employees.

In connection with changes in the organisation of production and labour, it is allowed to change the essential conditions of labour while continuing to work in the same speciality, qualification or position. Employees must be notified about changes in the essential conditions of labour - the system and amounts of remuneration, benefits, working hours, establishment or cancellation of part-time work, combination of professions, change of grades, job titles and others - no later than two months in advance. At least two months in advance. If the employer cannot change or maintain the previous essential conditions and the employee does not agree to continue working under the new conditions, the employment contract is terminated.

So, transfer to another job is a change in the nature and place of work established by the employment contract.

When moving or transferring to another job, an employee reassesses his/her existing professional qualities from the angle of their relevance to the new place of work, new labour function, different working conditions, and future relations of subordination and coordination. The unknown or fully learned is always a reason for rethinking and increasing the professional readiness of the employee to adapt and, in some cases, to survive in a new labour environment. It is at such a stage that the labour attitude of the participant of joint labour is strengthened or re-formed. Labour subordinated to the employer. From these positions "change of work" up to the change of speciality, qualification, and in some cases profession has a positive effect on the formation of personality, its labour self-realisation. A change of place, type of work is often a necessary condition for the ability to work, realisation of original qualities of a creative personality, the capabilities of an adaptive worker.

In terms of the duration of performing other work, all cases of transfers can be qualified into: 1) transfers to another permanent job; 2) transfers to another temporary job. Transfers to another permanent job at the same place of work are allowed only with the consent of the employee.

Transfer to another place of work can be an initiative of both the employee and the employer. But in a number of cases nowadays the employer himself offers the employee to transfer to another place of work. For example, in case of staff reduction, inconsistency with the position held, and the transfer in this way presupposes transfer to the position corresponding to the employee. In the absence of such a job, he should be offered another job.

The employer is also obliged to transfer to another job workers who, due to reduced capacity for work, are unable to perform their regular work duties properly. If there is no such regular work available at the time, they shall remain in their previous job until another job is available. If an employee refuses a transfer to another job, he or she may be dismissed with severance pay. Dismissal due to refusal of transfer may be permissible. If the employee does not wish to transfer to another job, and the employee's remaining at the previous job contradicts the medical conclusion. However, the reduced ability to work in the absence of proof of inconsistency of the work performed with the employee's health condition is not a ground for dismissal. In other cases, transfer to another job is the right, but not the obligation of the employer.

An employee's refusal to be transferred to another job on a permanent basis does not entail any legal consequences. Failure to comply with the employer's transfer order, given without the employee's consent, cannot be regarded as a violation of labour discipline and is not grounds for dismissal. If an employee is transferred to a permanent but lower-paid job, he or she is legally entitled to retain his or her previous salary for two months.

If it is a temporary transfer to another job not stipulated in the labour contract, it may be allowed with the consent of the employee. The only exceptions are transfers due to industrial necessity or downtime. Upon expiry of the temporary transfer period, employees are subject to compulsory reinstatement to their previous place of work.

Legislation also characterises the concept of industrial necessity.

Firstly, the transfer must be in the industrial interests of the enterprise ("industrial necessity for the enterprise"). This clarification is due to the fact that in departmental practice it was not uncommon for employees to be transferred to other enterprises in the interests of the latter.

Secondly, industrial necessity implies occurrence of exceptional circumstances of unforeseen nature affecting the course of production (e.g. natural disaster, industrial accident, accident, loss or damage of state or public property, etc.). Such transfers must prevent the occurrence of such circumstances or to eliminate their harmful effects.

Production necessity, which determines transfer to another job, also includes replacement of an absent employee due to his/her illness, leave, business trip (temporary substitution). The duration of such a transfer may not exceed one month within a calendar year (for other cases of transfers due to industrial necessity, the one-month period determines the maximum duration of a single transfer). The continuation of the transfer deadlines caused by the delayed return of the main employee is possible only with the consent of the substitute employee and with the preservation of pay guarantees. But the appointment of an employee to act in a vacant position is not allowed. This is possible only for a position, the appointment to which is made by a superior management body with subsequent approval.

Downtime is a frequent case of production necessity. Transfer to another job due to downtime is important in the fight for austerity, as downtime leads to lost working time, irrational use of labour force, and increased unproductive costs.

Transfer to another job as a result of idle time is made taking into account the speciality and qualification of the employee. In this case, as well as when temporarily replacing an absent employee, it is not allowed to transfer qualified workers and employees to unqualified jobs.

In case of transfer due to industrial necessity, payment is made according to the work performed, but not lower than the average earnings in the previous job.

In cases of refusal to transfer to another job due to industrial necessity or idle time without valid reasons may be considered as a violation of labour discipline.

Thus, transfer to another enterprise or another locality. Legislation on transfers for permanent work to another enterprise is based on the following principles: a) coordination of the transfer with the employee; b) reimbursement of expenses incurred by the employee in connection with the move to another locality; c) material incentives for transfers to work in those enterprises that are experiencing a shortage of personnel.

An employee's refusal to be transferred to another enterprise or to another locality does not entitle the employer to terminate the contract. Dismissal of an employee in these cases on the employer's initiative is possible only if there are other grounds provided for by law (e.g. staff reduction, incompatibility with the position held).

Analysing this labour form where the legislator thinks that the interests of the employee and the employer should be optimally combined. That is why transfer to another job is usually allowed with the written consent of the employee (part 1, article 71 of the Labour Code of the Russian Federation). Only upon written request or with written consent "an employee may be transferred to another employer for permanent work" (part 2 of Article 71 of the Labour Code of the RF). In this case, according to the legislator, the employment contract at the previous place of work is terminated (part 2 of Article 77 of the Labour Code of the RF).

If the legislator was consistent, then by recognising termination of the employment contract in case of change of place of work, he should have recognised termination of the employment contract also in cases of change of type of work, and even more so in cases of simultaneous change of type and place of work, even if with the same employer. Any transfer or relocation should be assessed on the basis of the common interests of the employees and the employer, the preservation of the enterprise, its competitiveness and profitability. The organisation is a place to work, for the employee to realise his professional capabilities, to generate income to support himself and his family. Not to worry about the prosperity of the enterprise for the employee is the risk of losing these opportunities, work, income, a worthy place in civil society, to join the ranks of the unemployed. Such a prospect always has a mobilising effect not only on the employee but also on the employer. Legislation as a kind of preventive measures provides for the possibility of changing the terms of the employment contract defined by the parties, related to changes in the organisational or technological conditions of work (Article 74 of the Labour Code of the Russian Federation), and in case of the possibility of mass dismissal of employees - in order to save jobs, with the opinion of the trade union organisation of the enterprise taken into account, to the regime of part-time working hours (working week) for a period of up to six months (part 5 of Article 74 of the Labour Code of the Russian Federation).

Such changes in the labour biography of an employee are always connected with reassessment of his/her attitude to work, production team, employer, awareness of common interests, formation of corporate culture in market conditions of economic management.

Chapter 3 Ways to address labour relations issues

Since the main and most important source of labour legislation is the Labour Code, it will already be possible to judge the general problems of labour legislation by considering its advantages and disadvantages.

In 2007, the Plenum of the Supreme Court of the Russian Federation adopted Resolution No. 2 "On the Application of the Labour Code of the Russian Federation by the Courts of the Russian Federation". You can read about some of the most relevant theoretical and practical problems of the application of the Labour Code of the Russian Federation below.

Since the adoption of the Labour Code of the Russian Federation, legal practitioners have had to independently interpret the Code's norms, many of which are characterised by uncertainty and ambiguity in their application. Moreover, not all articles of the Russian Labour Code comply with the norms of international labour law and the Constitution of the Russian Federation.

Firstly, Article 5 of the Labour Code of the Russian Federation does not directly single out the Constitution of the Russian Federation among other sources of labour legislation.

Secondly, the Labour Code of the RF does not answer the most important practical question: how should the law enforcer act in cases of contradictions between the Constitution of the RF and the Labour Code of the RF? Article 5 of the LC RF resolves only one type of hierarchical conflicts between the LC RF and other federal laws: "...in case of contradictions between this Code and other federal laws containing norms of labour law, this Code shall apply".

Thirdly, Article 10 of the Labour Code of the Russian Federation "Laws, other normative legal acts containing norms of labour law and norms of international law" merely reproduces part 4 of Article 15 of the Constitution of the Russian Federation without answering numerous practical questions. In this connection, paragraph 9 of the Resolution may be of the most important practical and theoretical significance. According to it, when considering labour cases, the court should take into account that by virtue of Article 15(1) and (4), Article 120 of the Constitution of the Russian Federation, and Article 11(1) of the Code of Civil Procedure of the Russian Federation, the court is obliged to resolve cases on the basis of the Constitution of the Russian Federation, generally recognised principles and norms of international law and international treaties of the Russian Federation, which are an integral part of its legal system. If, in resolving a labour dispute, the court finds that the normative legal act to be applied does not comply with the normative legal act having the greatest legal force, it decides in accordance with the normative legal act having the greatest legal force. When resolving labour disputes, courts must take into account the explanations of the Plenum of the Supreme Court of the Russian Federation given in resolutions No. 8 of 31 October 1995 "On Certain Issues of Application by Courts of the Constitution of the Russian Federation in the Execution of Justice" and No. 5 of 10 October 2003 "On the Application by Courts of General Jurisdiction of Universally Recognised Principles and Norms of International Law and International Treaties of the Russian Federation".

In practice, many disputes arise on issues related to the conclusion of a fixed-term labour contract. First of all, on the grounds stipulated in Article 59 of the Labour Code of the Russian Federation. For example, with age pensioners, persons working on a part-time basis, "temporary" employees, managers, deputy managers and chief accountants of organisations. Therefore, paragraph 15 of the Resolution is extremely relevant, according to which, when deciding on the validity of concluding a fixed-term labour contract with employees, it should be taken into account that such a contract is concluded when labour relations cannot be established for an indefinite period of time taking into account the nature of the work to be performed or the conditions of its performance, unless otherwise provided for by the Labour Code of the Russian Federation and other federal laws.

Since Article 59 of the Code provides only for the right and not the obligation of the employer to conclude a fixed-term employment contract in cases provided for by this provision, the employer may exercise this right provided that the general rules for concluding a fixed-term employment contract set out in Article 58 of the Labour Code are complied with

Article 136 of the Labour Code of the Russian Federation previously expressly provided: "The body considering a labour dispute has the right to take into account the gravity of the committed misconduct, the circumstances in which it was committed, the previous behaviour of the employee, his attitude to work, as well as the compliance of the disciplinary penalty with the gravity of the committed misconduct".

Unfortunately, the Labour Code of the Russian Federation does not contain such a norm. We believe that in this case there is a violation of part 2 of article 55 of the Constitution of the Russian Federation: "in the Russian Federation, no laws shall be issued that abolish or diminish human and civil rights and freedoms".

Given the extreme relevance of this problem for practice, the most important is para. 53 of the Resolution, according to which, by virtue of Article 46 (part 1) of the Constitution of the Russian Federation, which guarantees everyone judicial protection of their rights and freedoms, and the correlating provisions of international legal acts, in particular, Article 8 of the Universal Declaration of Human Rights, Article 6 (para. 1) of the International Covenant on Civil and Political Rights, the state is obliged to ensure the exercise of the right to judicial protection, which must be fair, competent, full and effective; taking this into account, the court must render not only a lawful, but also a reasoned decision, taking into account such general principles as the right to a fair trial, the right to a fair trial, and the right to a fair trial.

Since the right is an equal measure, the Plenum in paragraph 27 of the Resolution reasonably emphasised that the general legal principle of inadmissibility of abuse of right, enshrined, in particular, in part 3 of Article 17 of the Constitution of the Russian Federation, must be observed by the employee as well. For example, it is inadmissible for an employee to conceal his temporary disability at the time of his dismissal from work or the fact that he is a member of a trade union or the head (his deputy) of an elected trade union collegial body of the organisation. If the court establishes that the parties to a labour contract have abused their rights, the court may rule accordingly.

In practice, either deliberately or due to unprofessionalism, the evaluative concept of Article 75 of the Labour Code of the Russian Federation is interpreted incorrectly: "change of ownership of the organisation's property". Many people assume that "change of the owner of the organisation's property" occurs when there is a change of ownership of a share in a JSC or a share in an LLC. At the same time, the property transferred to LLC or JSC as contributions by their founders (participants), as well as the property acquired by these organisations, is the private property of LLC or JSC (Clause 3 of Article 213 of the Civil Code of the RF). The founders (participants) of an LLC or JSC have no rights in rem, they acquire only rights of obligation (Clause 2, Article 48 of the Civil Code of the Russian Federation).

A systematic interpretation of the Civil Code of the RF and the Labour Code of the RF allowed the Plenum to clarify in p. 32 of the Resolution that a change of ownership of an organisation's property should be understood as a transfer (transfer) of ownership of all of the organisation's property from one person to another person or other persons, in particular, in the privatisation of state or municipal property; in cases stipulated by p. 1 of Art. 66 and p. 1 of Art. 1 of Art. 66 and para. 3 of Art. 213 of the Civil Code of the Russian Federation, there is no change of the owner of the property.

Article 142 of the Labour Code of the Russian Federation, which provides: "In case of delay in payment of wages for more than 15 days, the employee has the right, after notifying the employer in writing, to suspend work for the entire period until the delayed amount is paid". In practice, at least two questions arose: must the employee go to work and is he or she entitled to receive wages in this case? In answer to the first question, the majority of judges of the Supreme Court of the Russian Federation considered that since Article 142 of the Labour Code of the Russian Federation does not oblige an employee who has suspended work to be present at his workplace during the period of time for which he suspended work, taking into account that violation of the terms of payment of wages - or payment of wages not in full amount - refers to forced labour (Article 4 of the Labour Code of the Russian Federation), so the employee has the right not to go to work until the delayed amount is paid. The Draft Resolution provided three options for answering the second question.

The first is to recover wages, as the suspension of work on the basis of Article 142 of the Labour Code of the Russian Federation is a form of self-protection by the employee of his right to perform the work provided for in the employment contract, timely and full payment of wages.

The second is to recover wages only for those workers who were present at work, because they were deprived of the possibility of receiving other income in lieu of wages during the period in question, not at their place of work.

The third option is to deny the claim for recovery of wages due to the fact that such a possibility is not provided for by the Labour Code of the RF. It seems that the last variant of the answer is more reasonable, because the rights of both citizens and legal entities can be limited only by federal law (part 3 of article 55 of the Constitution of the Russian Federation, paragraph 2 of article 1 of the Civil Code of the Russian Federation). Article 142 of the Labour Code of the RF does not provide the court with such an opportunity. Moreover, we cannot speak about a gap in Article 142 of the Labour Code of the RF, as there is Article 236 of the Labour Code of the RF, which establishes material liability of the employer for delayed payment of wages - recovery of interest (monetary compensation) rather than wages.

Quite reasonably, the majority of the Plenum participants came to the conclusion: the answer to the second question falls within the competence of law-making bodies, not the court.

Perhaps, due to the numerous controversial articles in the Labour Code of the Russian Federation from the point of view of international labour law and the Constitution of the Russian Federation, not all relevant problems of application of labour law were reflected in the text of the adopted Resolution. This was understood both by the drafters of the draft Resolution and by the judges of the Supreme Court of the Russian Federation who voted at the Plenum. In this regard, the Plenum of the Supreme Court of the Russian Federation made a fundamental decision: work on the interpretation of the Labour Code of the Russian Federation should be continued.

Another problem related to the protection of labour rights is the insufficient use of international legal norms by the judiciary. Despite the large volume of Russian legislation and the often objective inability of judges to apply specific international acts, the highest court of the country points to the need to use international legal norms in the administration of justice. In the case of labour relations, it is sometimes difficult to follow this recommendation because judges do not have the texts of ratified conventions of the International Labour Organization. It is noteworthy that courts of general jurisdiction rarely use international labour rights standards as direct regulators when considering specific cases. A survey of judges has shown that more than 50 per cent of judges, on the basis of practical expediency and the existence of a large body of national legislation, which should not inherently contradict international instruments, apply international norms only when there are obvious conflicts between the relevant norms. In addition, this practice is also explained by the fact that the Russian Federation has not yet accumulated sufficient experience in applying these norms. It is understandable that this may lead to insufficiently effective legal protection.

Conclusion

The main conclusions of the paper are as follows:

1. As a branch of law, labour law is, first of all, a system of legal norms established by the state with the participation of employees and trade unions, which regulate labour relations of employees and other relations closely related to them. The norms of labour law determine the procedure for the emergence and termination of labour legal relations, the mode of work of employees, fixed internal labour regulations (i.e. rules of conduct at work) and other norms.

The subject matter of labour law is social relations arising from the application of employees' labour, i.e. direct labour relations and certain other relations closely related to them and set out in Article 4 of the Labour Code. Such relations may precede labour relations, derive from labour relations or accompany labour relations, but all of them are regulated by labour legislation.

Labour relations are characterised by the following features that distinguish them from other types of legal relations:

- The subject of labour relations is the employee, he is included in the the staff of the enterprise, i.e. enrolled in the staff or list of the enterprise.

- An employee performs a specific labour function, it is means that throughout his employment with the employer he performs work in a particular occupation and position.

- The work is performed under the conditions of a specific labour regime,
i.e. the employee is subject to the employer's internal labour regulations.

2. Types of labour relations: relations based on an employment contract; relations based on membership in a collective.

The labour law system includes institutes:

- collective bargaining and agreements;

- employment of citizens;

- of the labour contract;

- working hours;

time off;

- of labour rationing;

- wages (labour remuneration);
- of labour discipline;

- material liability of the parties to a labour relationship;

- benefits for those who combine work and study;

- labour protection, supervision and control over compliance with labour law

legislation; labour disputes.

3. The institute of labour disputes also includes two relatively independent groups of norms - regulating, on the one hand, individual and, on the other hand, collective labour disputes. The labour rights of workers are part of the opportunities guaranteed by the state in the sphere of labour activity. They allow all workers to use freely and without discrimination their full human potential to meet their material needs and to ensure the interests of their families. The value of labour rights lies in the fact that they enable citizens to fulfil themselves in the labour sphere in the manner permitted by the State. It is therefore not so much the proclamation and enshrinement of the relevant rights in the Constitution and existing legislation that is important, but rather the filling of them with concrete content and the establishment of guarantees for their proper realisation and protection. Judicial protection is the main guarantee of the protection of labour rights and their non-violability. Judicial protection is primarily aimed at protecting against any violations by both State bodies and private individuals.

List of references

1. History of domestic state and law (in 2 volumes; volume 2) / edited by O.I. Chistyakov. Moscow: Yurist, 2013 - 544 p.

2. Commentary to the Labour Code of the Russian Federation (ed. by K.N. Gusov) - Moscow: "TC Velby", "Prospect Publishing House", 2013 - 544 p.

3. Kurenoy A.M. Legal regulation of termination of labour contract // Legislation, 2002, No. 12 P. 42-48, 2014, №1, с. 28 - 34

4. Tolkunova V.N., Gusov K.N. Labour Law M.: TC VELBI, 2006 - 320 p.

5. Khnykin G.V. Collective agreement // Legislation, 2015, No. 11, pp. 51 -61

6. Khnykin G.V. Internal labour regulations // Legislation, 2015, No. 12, pp. 46 -52

7. Chikanova L. Labour discipline // Khozyaistvo i pravo, 2012, № 9, p.16 - 32.

8. Chikanova L.A. Labour contract // Khozyaistvo i pravo, 2016, No. 5, pp. 10 - 29, No. 6, pp. 12-26

Table of contents

I want morebooks!

Buy your books fast and straightforward online - at one of world's fastest growing online book stores! Environmentally sound due to Print-on-Demand technologies.

Buy your books online at
www.morebooks.shop

Kaufen Sie Ihre Bücher schnell und unkompliziert online – auf einer der am schnellsten wachsenden Buchhandelsplattformen weltweit! Dank Print-On-Demand umwelt- und ressourcenschonend produziert.

Bücher schneller online kaufen
www.morebooks.shop

Printed by Books on Demand GmbH, Norderstedt / Germany